A Miracle TODAY!

Old Testament and Inspirational Miracles

Written by:
Larry S. Glover

Published by:
Childlike Faith Children's Books

Illustrated by:
Neel Solanki

This book is dedicated to all of the
children who believe in miracles,
and in miracles today.

Published by Childlike Faith Children's Books
2012 Wages Way
Jacksonville, FL 32218
Childlikefaithchildrensbooks.com

Author: Larry S. Glover
Illustration: Neel Solanki
Production: ABC Book Publishers, Inc.
Graphic Design: Jeanine Quinn
Editor: Kimberly Benton

Print ISBN: 978-1-7331584-9-7
E-book ISBN: 978-1-7355149-8-7
Library of Congress Control Number: 2020932021

Printed in the United States of America

10 9 8 7 6 5 4 3 2 1

Do you want to see a miracle?
You only have to pray and say,
"Dear God show me a miracle."
And he will show you...

A Miracle Today!

The word "miracle" comes from God and for him,
they are not so hard.

Genesis 1:1 The very first miracle was in the beginning.

The Grand Canyon was found in 1200 BC.
Now, that's pretty old! Much older than you and me.

That's A Miracle Today!

God said, "LET THERE BE LIGHT" and now we can see.
This was a miracle from God, for you and me.

Genesis 1:2 The miracle of light.

When I wake up, it's a new day I see.
I thank God for making it and letting me be me!

That's A Miracle Today!

The miracle of creation is when all things were birthed.
That is why God took his time to make the planet earth.

Genesis 1:9-12 The miracle of how all things were created.

When dinosaurs walked the whole ground shook.
They left big footprints with every step they took.

That's A Miracle Today!

Then there was the miracle of the plants, the stars, sun and moon.
In a few more days, people would be coming soon.

Genesis 1:14 -19 The miracle of the sun, moon, and solar system.

The earth spins around at an amazing speed.
Gravity keeps us from falling and gives us what we need.

That's A Miracle Today!

Next, there is the miracle of water, animals, food and plants.
We can't forget even the smallest ant!

Genesis 1:20-25
The miracle of animals, bugs and insects that can walk, fly, swim and crawl.

Butterflies are a beautful sight for our eyes.
These are little miracles, so be surprised when they fly by!

That's A Miracle Today!

5

After God saw that all of his work was good,
he made man because he could.

Genesis 1:26-31 / Genesis 2:7
The miracle of the first man.

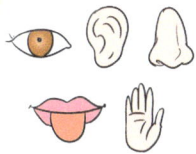

We can SEE, FEEL, HEAR, SMELL and TASTE.
We can do these things because of God's grace.

That's A Miracle Today!

Adam and Eve lived in the garden.
God gave them what they needed and helped them get started.

Genesis 2:7-23
The miracle of the man and the woman and all mankind.

How do we get a chicken from an egg?
Add feathers, and a beak, two feet and two legs!

That's A Miracle Today!

Noah made a boat, it was long and tall.
He saved his family and the animals before the rain began to fall.

Genesis 5:31 and Genesis 10:1
The miracle of a big boat that saved the people and animals.

Our brain gives us the power to think, and read.
Just use your brain, that's all you need.

That's A Miracle Today!

Abraham and Sarah had a child when they were very old. God blessed them with this miracle birth, and that's how the story was told.

Genesis 18:11-14
The miracle of how God blessed two very old people with a child.

A baby is born so beautiful and so sweet,
and they look so peaceful when they are fast asleep.

That's A Miracle Today!

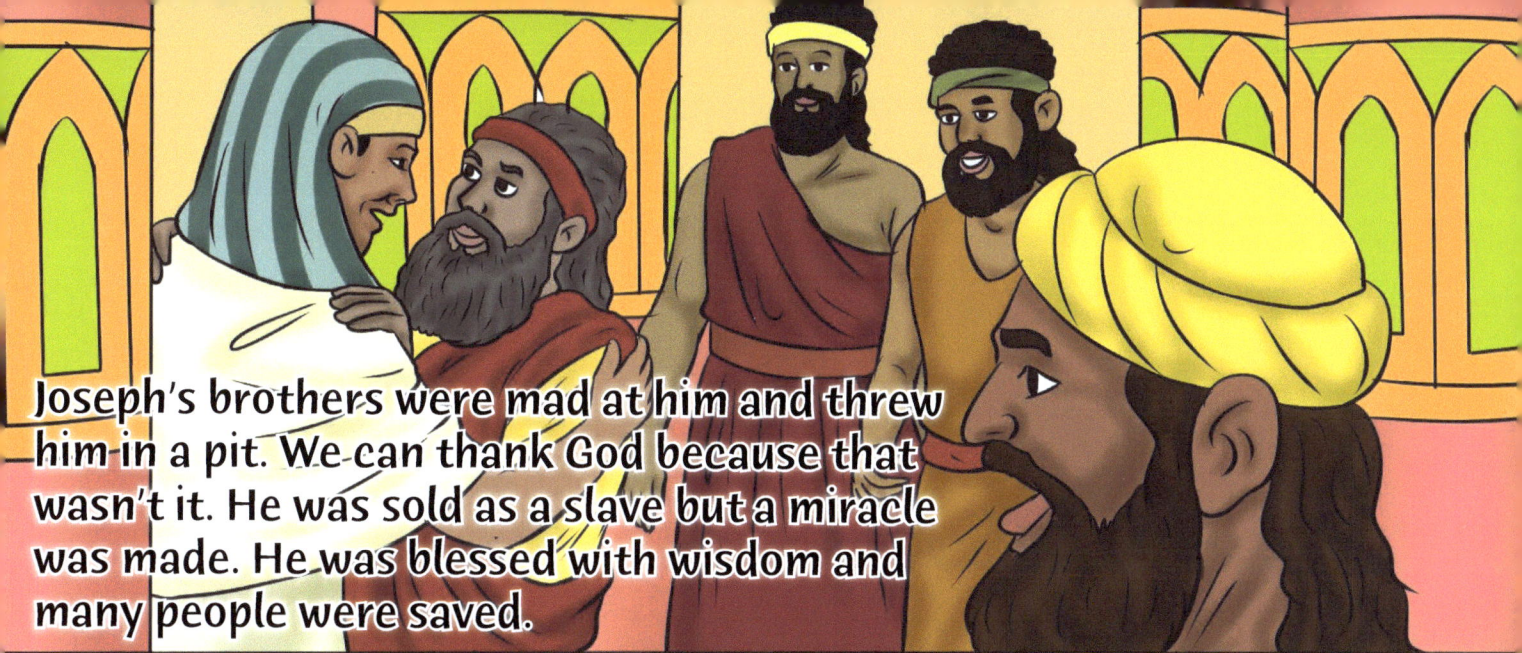

Joseph's brothers were mad at him and threw him in a pit. We can thank God because that wasn't it. He was sold as a slave but a miracle was made. He was blessed with wisdom and many people were saved.

Genesis 41:56 and Genesis 42:2
The miracle of Joseph saves his family and all the people.

Miracles are gifts that come our way. They can help those in need and can come any day.

That's A Miracle Today!

God told Moses to part the red sea.
God did this miracle to set his people free.

Exodus 14:21
The miracle of the sea opening up so Gods people could be saved.

God made this animal called a Giraffe.
If you look at it long enough you might even laugh!

That's A Miracle Today!

11

God's people were in the desert and they had no food to eat. Bread and birds fell from the sky- "IT WAS A MIRACLE" and a tasty treat.

Exodus 16:4-17
The miracle of food coming down from the sky to feed the hungry people.

SOAP was invented from a simple peanut and so many other cool things that would make you say, "No Way!"

That's A Miracle Today!

12

God wrote his word on tablets of stone,
so his people could know him
and carry on.

Exodus 20:2-17
The miracle of God writing his word on stone.

Each hour of the day, moves us forward in every way.

That's A Miracle Today!

God gave a donkey the power to speak, and to tell a man what God said and what God thinks.

Exodus 22:21-35
The miracle of an animal talking to a man... WOW!

Hello

We have birds that can talk, laugh and sing.
Don't you know God can do anything?

That's A Miracle Today!

It was a miracle when
God covered Moses eyes.
There was a cleft in the rock
where Moses would hide.

Exodus 33:22-23
The miracle of God, Moses and the mountain.

Televisions are amazing machines.
They can show us how to follow our dreams.

That's A Miracle Today!

God's people cried out to Moses, "THERE IS NO WATER IN THIS LAND!" God told Moses to hit the rock, and Moses hit the rock again.

Numbers 20:22
The miracle of thirsty people. Moses hit the rock ad water came out.

The water moves at Niagara Falls and never stops.
It is strong and mighty, and flows down from the top.

That's A Miracle Today!

It was at the battle of Jericho where God's army marched around.
They made so much noise that the walls came tumbling down.

Joshua 6:6-20
The miracle of so much noise that walls came tumbling down.

Snowflakes are so pretty when they fall from the sky.
You can even make a snowman three piles high.

That's A Miracle Today!

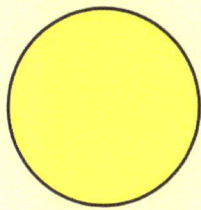

God wanted his people to listen and do his will, so he showed them a sign and made the sun stand still.

Joshua 10:12-14
The miracle of the sun standing still for a full day.

How does cotton grow? Nobody knows.
Cotton makes so many things, and it even makes our clothes.

That's A Miracle Today!

Sampson was strong and his shoulders were broad.
He was a mighty man, but the miracles came from God.

Judges 16:1-31
The miracle of the man who was very, very, very strong.

The ancient Pyramids are so big, so wide and so old.
They are still here today and many stories have been told.

That's A Miracle Today!

19

God chose Ruth, in the bible, to carry out his plan and it was through her family, that God brought forth the Son of man.

Ruth 2:1-23
The miracle of how our Lord and savior came to be the son of God.

God made heaven and he wants us to know that this is the place where he wants us to go.

That's A Miracle Today!

David used a rock to bring Goliath to the ground. Then, the whole army ran and were nowhere to be found!

1 Samuel 17:41-52
The miracle of the young boy defeating the big giant with a rock.

The paper that we use is made from trees. Grab a pencil and paper and draw whatever you please.

That's A Miracle Today!

God chose Queen Ester to save his people because the miracle from God showed the King who was evil.

Ester 7:1-6
The miracle of how the king was told the truth.

Science is one way that we discover many things.
God shows us each day what science really means.

That's A Miracle Today!

"Into the fiery furnace!" said the angry king because 3 Hebrew boys wouldn't bow to their knees.

The flames were hot no doubt, and it was a miracle from God that brought the 3 boys out.

Daniel 3:1-30
The miracle of the 3 Hebrew boys saved from the fire.

A lighting bug has a light that glows on its bottom. God put the light there, that's how they got um.

That's A Miracle Today!

23

God's servant Daniel was thrown into the lion's den.
It was a miracle from God that made Daniel and the lions friends.

Daniel 6:12-28
The miracle of the man who sat down with lions.

God gave man an idea to create more light.
The light bulb is one reason why a room can be so bright.

That's A Miracle Today!

God chose a great big fish so his plan would not fail.
That's why Jonah spent 3 whole days in the belly of a whale.

Jonah 1:1-17
The miracle of how God used a great big fish to put a man back on dry land.

A whale is big, mighty and strong.
They live in the ocean and they live very long.

That's A Miracle Today!

We have talked about
miracles in every way.
Now just look around
and you will see...

A Miracle Today!

What is a Miracle?

A miracle is something
that we really cannot say
how it happens.

We can only say, *"WOW, that's a miracle!"*
when we see it.

Like two, three, or even four children that are
born at the same time and they **all** look alike
WOW, that's a miracle!

Animals in the air, in the water and on the ground,
WOW, that's a miracle, too!

It's like the first car that was ever made, someone
had a dream and then created a design.

A miracle is a surprise, a mystery, a marvel or a
wonder from something Devine. This whole world is
a miracle, just look around you and you will see…

A Miracle Today!

What miracles have you seen today?

28

THE KIDS EMPOWERMENT SERIES

Order other books by Larry S. Glover:

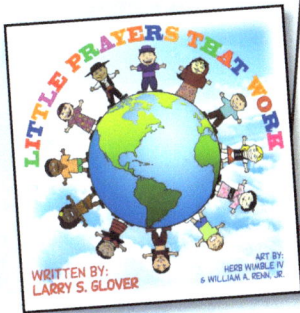

Little Prayers That Work

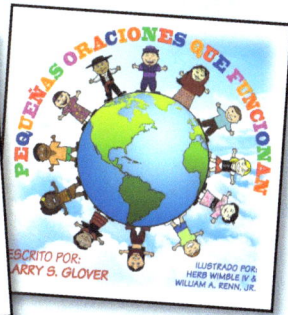

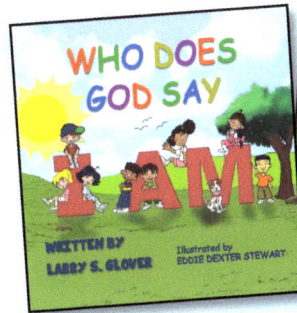

Who Does God Say I Am

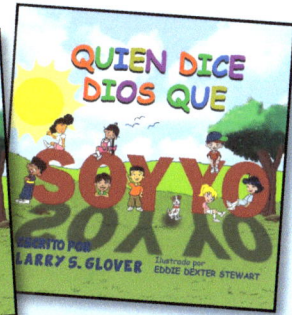

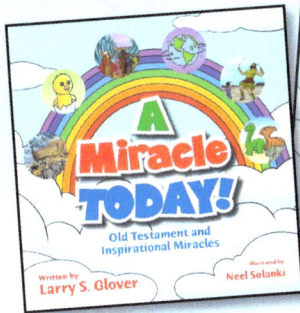

A Miracle Today - Old Testament

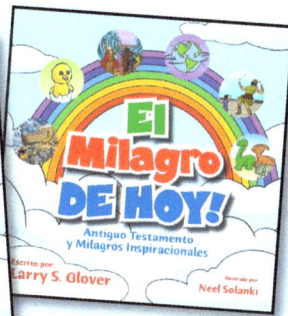

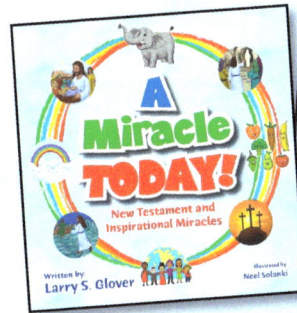

A Miracle Today - New Testament

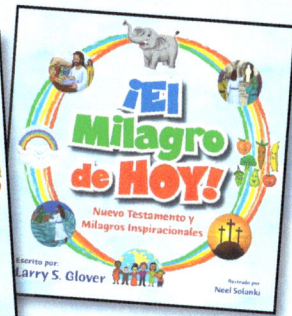

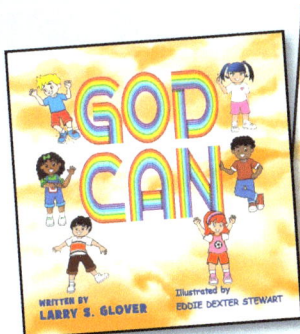

GOD CAN

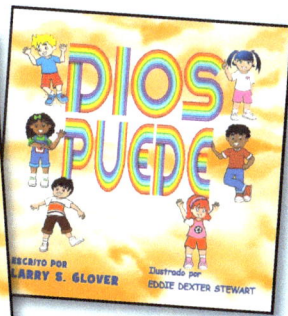

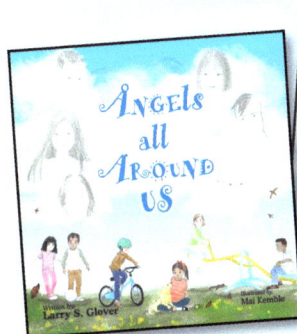

Angels All Around Us

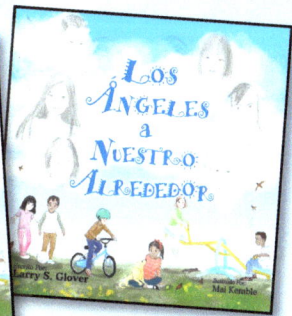

Coming Soon:
A Place Where We Can Go
God is Love

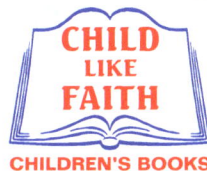

CHILD LIKE FAITH
CHILDREN'S BOOKS

Available in English and Spanish
on Amazon.com
www.childlikefaithchildrensbooks.com

THE KID'S VALUE SERIES

Order other books by Larry S. Glover:

Available in English and Spanish.

Be Good

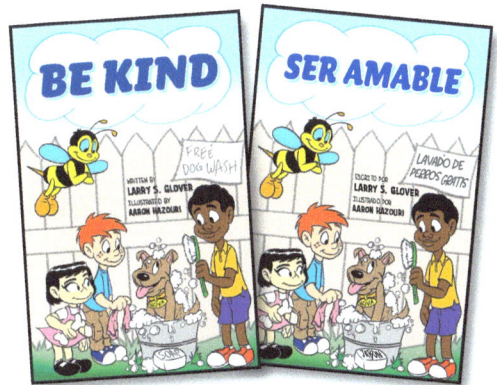

Be Kind

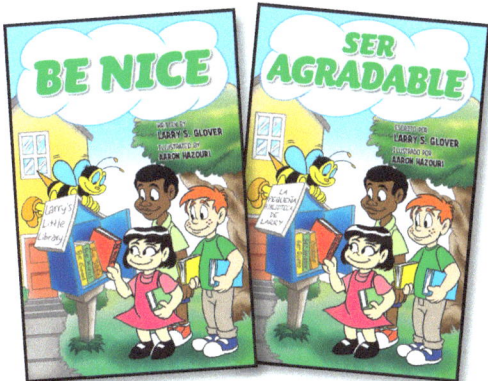

Be Nice

Be Safe

www.childlikefaithchildrensbooks.com

www.ingramcontent.com/pod-product-compliance
Lightning Source LLC
Chambersburg PA
CBHW042104040426
42448CB00002B/131

* 9 7 8 1 7 3 3 1 5 8 4 9 7 *